Bluegrass Complete

Catalog No. 07-1020
ISBN #1-56922-001-8

Executive Selling Agent:
CREATIVE CONCEPTS PUBLISHING CORPORATION
410 Bryant Circle, Box 848
Ojai, California 93024

CONTENTS

CONTENTS

CONTENTS

CONTENTS

BILL MONROE

Sitting from left: DON RENO, BILL MONROE and LESTER FLATT
Standing from left: JAMES MONROE, MAC WISEMAN, BILL YATES,
RALPH STANLEY and JIMMY MARTIN

JIM & JESSE McREYNOLDS

RALPH AND CARTER STANLEY

GRANDPA JONES

EARL SCRUGGS

CARL STORY

EARL SCRUGGS REVUE

BILL MONROE & LESTER FLATT

MAC WISEMAN

JOHN HARTFORD

THE OSBORNE BROTHERS

DOC WATSON

DON RENO, BILL HARRELL & THE TENNESSEE CUTUPS

BILL MONROE, RALPH RINZLER, BILL KEITH AND
DEL McCOURY

BLUEGRASS BANJO CHORD CHART

G TUNING
G-DGBD

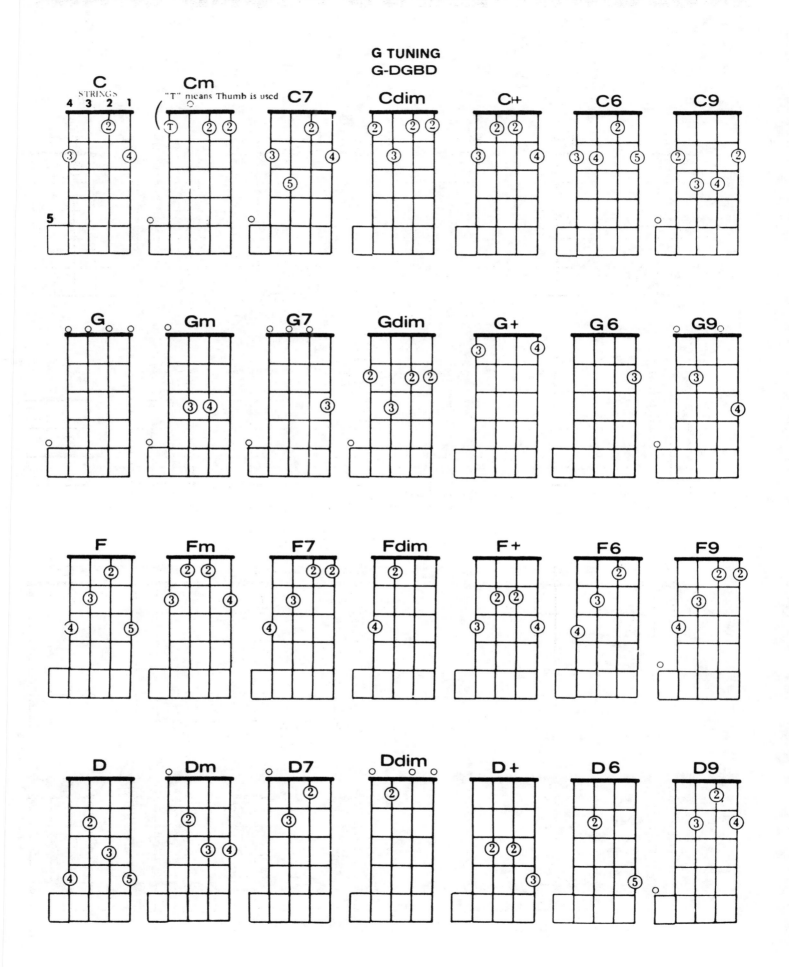

BLUEGRASS BANJO CHORD CHART

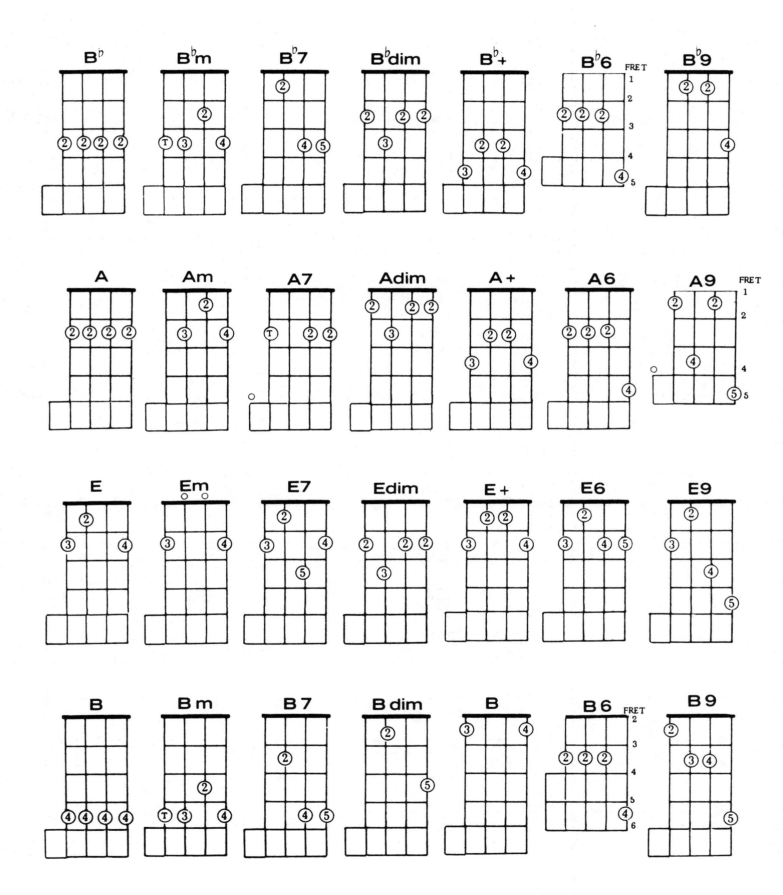

AMERICAN TRILOGY
DIXIE/BATTLE HYMN OF THE REPUBLIC/ALL MY TRIALS·

Traditional

ARKANSAS TRAVELER

Arranged and Adapted by
SLIM MARTIN

Medium Tempo

Oh, once up-on a time in Ar-kan-sas, An old man sat in his lit-tle cab-in door, And he

fid-dled at a tune that he liked to hear, A jol-ly old __ tune that he played by ear. It was

rain - ing hard but the fid-dler did-n't care, He sawed a - way at the pop-u-lar air, Though his

roof - tree leaked like a wa - ter-fall, That did-n't seem to both - er the man at all.

A traveller was riding by that day,
And stopped to hear him a-fiddling away;
The cabin was afloat and his feet were wet,
But still the old man didn't seem to fret.
    So the stranger said, "Now the way it seems to me,
    You'd better mend your roof," said he.
    But the old man said as he played away:
    "I couldn't mend it now, it's a rainy day."

The traveller replied, "That's all quite true,
But this, I think is the thing for you to do;
Get busy on a day that is fair and bright,
Then patch the old roof till it's good and tight."
    But the old man kept on a-playing at his reel,
    And tapped the ground with his leathery heel.
    "Get along," said he, "for you give me a pain—
    My cabin never leaks when it doesn't rain!"

Arkansas Traveller 2-2

BAD COMPANY

By TOM WILLS

D   **G**   **D**

tired _____ Of home and all of my friends, _____ I

G   **Em**   **G**   **D**   **A**   **A7**   **D**

know I won't be ad - mired, _____ The way my sto - ry ends. _____

2. I said farewell to lov'd ones,
   And in a far distant town,
   I joined the worst of companions,
   My morals went 'way, 'way down.
   We would steal to buy more liquor,
   We lived by breaking the laws,
   And I sank lower and lower,
   Bad company was the cause.

3. I met a fair young maiden,
   My love was really quite strong,
   But in my manner of courting,
   I did what was truly wrong.
   She advised me of a secret,
   That I a father would be,
   I stabbed her twice with a dagger,
   And she was gone from me.

4. So I was brought to justice,
   As now you clearly can see,
   My life was ruined forever,
   Because of bad company.
   And so I await the scaffold,
   My days are not very long.
   You'll be forgetting the singer,
   But don't forget the song.

BANKS OF THE OHIO

Adapted by
WOODY HAYES

Banks Of The Ohio-2

BEAUTIFUL BROWN EYES

Adapted by
BILL BRENNER

BEFORE I MET YOU

Arranged and Adapted by
SLIM MARTIN

Medium Tempo

I thought I had seen pret - ty girls in my time, That was be-

fore I met you._____ I nev - er saw one that I

want - ed for mine. That was be - fore I met you._____

Chorus:

2. I wanted to ramble and always be free,
   That was before I met you.
   I said that no woman could ever hold me,
   That was before I met you.
   Chorus

3. They tell me I must reap just what I have sown,
   Darling, I hope that's not true.
   Once I made plans about living alone,
   That was before I met you.
   Chorus

BLACK-EYED SUSIE

Arranged and Adapted by
SLIM MARTIN

Lively

Verse: All I want in this cre - a - tion, Pret - ty lit - tle wife and a big plan - ta - tion.

Chorus: Hey, pret - ty lit - tle Black - eyed Su - sie,

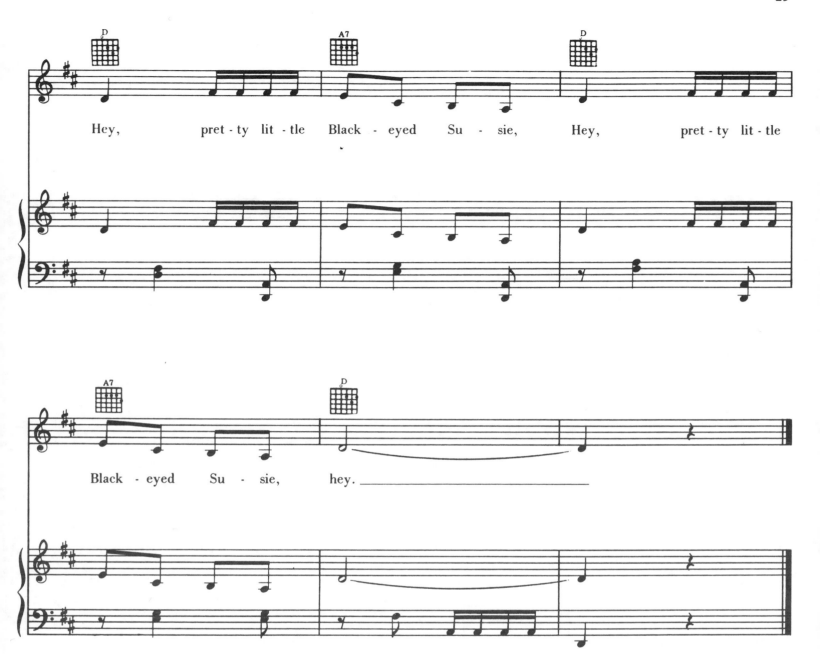

All I need to make me happy,
Two little boys to call me pappy. *Chorus*

Up Red Oak and down salt water,
Some old man gonna lose his daughter. *Chorus*

Black-eyed Susie went huckleberry pickin',
The boys got drunk and Susie took a lickin'. *Chorus*

Some got drunk and some got boozy,
I went home with Black-eyed Susie. *Chorus*

Black-eyed Susie's about half grown,
Jumps on a man like a dog on a bone. *Chorus*

Love my wife, I love my baby,
Love my biscuits sopped in gravy. *Chorus*

Black-Eyed Susie 2-2

BRING BACK MY WANDERING BOY

By SONNY LEWIS

2. Out in the hallway there stands an empty chair,
   And an old pair of shoes that once he did wear.
   Empty is the cradle that once he loved so well,
   Oh, how I miss him no tongue can tell.
   Chorus

3. Search till you find him and bring him back to me,
   Far, far away, wherever he may be.
   Tell him it's mother with faded cheeks and hair,
   She's at the old home awaiting him there.
   Chorus

Bring Back My Wandering Boy 2-2

BUDDY, WON'T YOU ROLL DOWN THE LINE

By JACK PORTER

Lively

Every Monday morning they get you out on time,
March you down to Lone Rock just to look into that mine.
March you down to Lone Rock to look into that hole,
Very last words the captain say, "You better get your pole".

The beans they are half done, the bread is not so well,
The meat it is all burnt up and the coffee's black as heck,
But when you get your task done, you're glad to come to call,
For anything you get to eat, it tastes good done or raw.

CARELESS LOVE

Adapted by
WOODY HAYES

CARRY ME BACK TO OLD VIRGINNY

Words and Music by
JAMES BLAND

CHILLY WINDS

Adapted by
BILL BRENNER

2. I'm goin' where the cold won't chill my bones, my sweet baby,
   I'm goin' where the cold won't chill my bones,
   When I'm gone to my long lonesome home.

3. I'm goin' where the folks all know me well, my sweet baby,
   I'm goin' where the folks all know me well, my sweet baby,
   When I'm gone to my long lonesome home.

4. Now, who will be your honey when I'm gone, my sweet baby,
   Now, who will be your honey when I'm gone, my sweet baby,
   When I'm gone to my long lonesome home.

CINDY

by TOM WILLS

Chorus:

Get a - long home, CIN - DY, CIN - DY, Get a - long

home, CIN - DY, CIN - DY, Get a - long

home, CIN - DY, CIN - DY, I'll

mar - ry you some day.

2. I
3. I   day.
4. I

Fine

Cindy — 2

CRAWDAD

By PHIL DORSEY

CRIPPLE CREEK

By
CHESTER BURNAM

CUMBERLAND GAP

Arranged and Adapted by
SLIM MARTIN

Mmm

'way down yon - der in Cum - ber - land Gap.

2. Cumberland Gap is a noted place,
   Three kinds of water to wash your face.
   Chorus

3. The first white man in Cumberland Gap
   Was Doctor Walker, an English chap.
   Chorus

4. Daniel Boone on Pinnacle Rock,
   He killed Injuns with his old flintlock.
   Chorus

5. Lay down, boys, and take a little nap,
   Fo'teen miles to the Cumberland Gap.
   Chorus

CUMBERLAND MOUNTAIN DEER CHASE

By TIM MORGAN

Moderately

Rover, Rover, see him, see him,
Rover, Rover, catch him, catch him,
Away and away we're bound for the mountain,
Away to the chase, away, away.

See there the wild deer, trembling, panting,
Trembling panting, trembling panting,
One moment pausing, no longer standing,
Away to the chase, away, away.

The Cumberland Mountain Deer Chase 2-2

DARLIN' COREY

Adapted by
CHARLOTTE GRAY

1. Wake up, wake up, DAR - LING COR - EY, What makes you sleep so sound? The rev - e - nue of - fi - cer's a - com - in' for to tear your still house down.

DELIA'S GONE
(ONE MORE ROUND)

Adapted by
JOE COLE

1. Miss De - lia, she two - timed her to - ny Sat - ur - day night, And
2. He brought her a cock - tail, the ver - y best _____ in the town, But

on this date, she met her fate, He shot her down at sight, DE - LIA
she re - fused to down the shot and so he shot her down, DE - LIA

GONE, One more round, DE - LIA GONE! _____ { DE - LIA GONE, One more
GONE, One more round, DE - LIA GONE! _____

3. He wanted to marry
   But she preferred to be loose,
   She did not want a goose to cook
   And so he cooked her goose.
   Delia gone, one more round,
   Delia gone! (Chorus)

4. So Tony was locked up,
   The judge refused to set bail,
   For such a crime, he should do time,
   Say, 99 years in jail.
   Delia gone, one more round,
   Delia gone! (Chorus)

5. Then Tony said "Thank You",
   "Your honor treated me fine."
   He knew the judge could well have said:
   Nine hundred ninety - nine.
   Delia gone, one more round,
   Delia gone! (Chorus)

DIXIE

By
DAN EMMET

I — wish I was — in the land of cot - ton, Old times there are
In — Dix - ie Land — Where — I was born in, Ear - ly on one

not for - got - ten Look a - way, Look a - way, Look a - way Dix - ie Land.
frost - y morn - in'

Then I wish I was in Dix - ie Hoo - ray, Hoo - ray! In

FOLLOW THE DRINKING GOURD

Adapted by
SONNY DAVIS

FOGGY MOUNTAIN TOP

By JERRY VAN PELT

Foggy Mountain Top 3-2

mine, there's some-thing I want you to tell her:

tell her not to be wast-ing her time

run-ning a-round with some oth-er fel-ler. _____

Oh, she's caused me to weep and she's caused me to moan,
She caused me to leave my home;
The lonesome pines and the good old times,
I'm on my way back home.

Oh, if I'd only listened to what my mama said,
I would not have been there today
Lying around this old jail cell,
Just a-weeping my poor life away.

CORRINA, CORRINA

by SAM HOPKINS

GEORGIA STOCKADE

Adapted by
BILL BRENNER

THE GREAT SPECKLED BIRD

By
REV. EARL OSBORN

THE HOUSE OF THE RISING SUN

Adapted by
ART SUMMIT

I AM A PILGRIM

by LESTER McGRATH

I got a mother, a sister and a brother,
Who have gone to that sweet land,
I'm determined to go and see them,
   good Lord,
All over on that distant shore.

As I go down to that river Jordan,
Just to bathe my weary soul,
If I could touch but the hem of His
   garment, good Lord,
Well, I believe it would make me whole.

I'M GOING BACK TO OLD KENTUCKY

By PHIL GREEN

Smoothly

When I left old Ken - tuck - y, ___ Lin - da

kissed me and she cried. ___ I told her that ___ I would not

wan - der, ___ I'd be back by and by. ___ I'm go - ing

Chorus:

2. Linda Lou, she is a beauty,
   Those pretty brown eyes, I loved so well.
   I'm going back to old Kentucky,
   Never more to say farewell.
   Chorus

3. Linda Lou, you know I love you,
   I long for you each night and day.
   When the roses bloom in old Kentucky,
   I'll be coming back to stay.
   Chorus

I'm Going Back to Old Kentucky 2-2

I NEVER WILL MARRY

Tenderly

by SUSANNE PERRY

They say that love's ____ a gen - tle thing, ____ But it's on - ly brought me pain; ____ For the on - ly man I ____

I Never Will Marry 2-2

IN THE PINES

Arranged and Adapted by
SLIM MARTIN

The long-est train I ev-er saw, Went down that Georg-ia line. The en-gine passed at six o'-clock, And cab passed by at

nine.　In The　Pines,　In The　Pines,　Where the　sun　nev-er

shines,　And we　shiv - er when the　cold　wind __ blows. _____

2. I asked my captain for the time of day,
   He said he throwed his watch away.
   A long steel ram and a short cross tie,
   I'm on my way back home.
   Chorus

3. Little girl, little girl, what have I done,
   That makes you treat me so?
   You caused me to weep, you caused me to mourn,
   You caused me to leave my home.
   Chorus

In The Pines 2-2

JESSE JAMES

By
WOODY HAYES

JOHN HARDY

Adapted by
WOODY HAYES

3. John Hardy might have lived as a free man today,
   Except for one mistake that he made,
   He went for to see if his fam'ly was O.K.,
   And the law was a-waitin' out in the shade, Oh Lord!
   And the law was a law that had to be paid.

4. John Hardy called himself just a fair-fightin' man,
   He said he had good reason to kill.
   He once ripped an arm from saloonkeeper, Dan,
   'Cause he sold watered whiskey out of a still, Oh Lord!
   Hardy bought watered whiskey out of a still.

5. John Hardy spoke these words with a noose 'round his neck,
   "My absence won't make anyone grieve.
   If this be the price, guess I'll have to pay the check,
   But I lost 'cause a card was up in his sleeve, Oh Lord!
   And John Hardy, he 'lows no card in a sleeve."

John Hardy — 2

JOHN HENRY

By
WOODY HAYES

Heavily

1. When JOHN
(2. JOHN _____)
(3. JOHN _____)

HEN - RY was a lit - tle ba - by, All he
HEN - RY, speak - ing to the fore - man, Said "A
HEN - RY had a lit - tle off - spring, And he

ev - er want - ed for a toy, Was the
man should prove him - self a man, And be
took him gent ly on his knee, And he

lit - tle kitch - en ham - mer, ham - mer, ham - mer,
fore I'd let your steam drill beat me down, I'll
hugged him and he kissed him, while he said: My

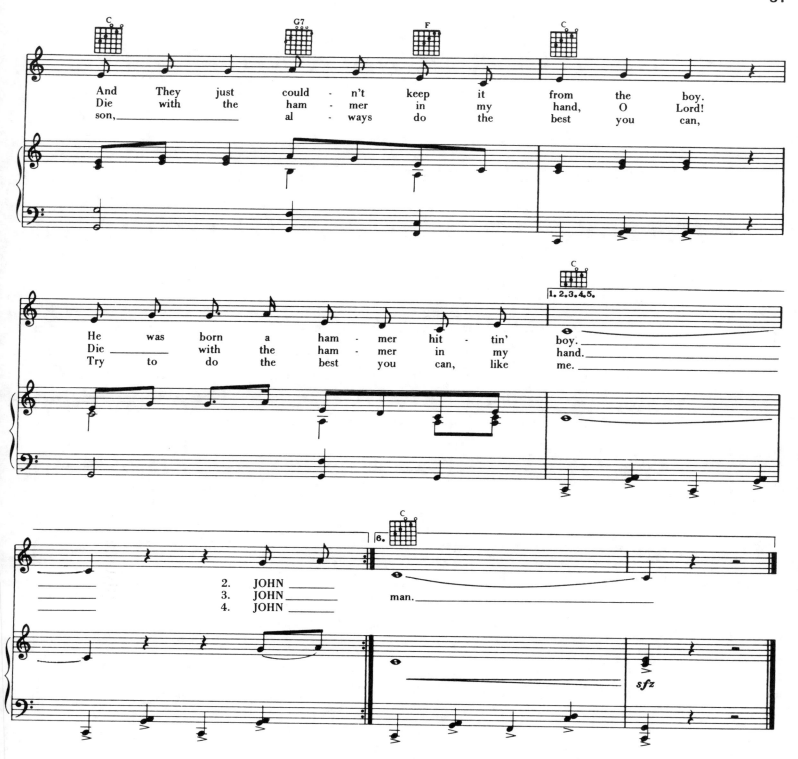

4. John Henry took a heavy hammer,
   And, beside the steam drill he did stand.
   He was faster than the drill, but oh! alas!
   He died with the hammer in his hand, O Lord!
   Died with the hammer in his hand.

5. So they took John Henry to the graveyard,
   And they laid him down into the sand,
   And when any locomotive passed the grave,
   'Tis said the engineer would look and say:
   There lies a steel-drivin' man.

6. John Henry, he's an inspiration,
   To the men whose hands are born for toil,
   Even in this day and age of automation,
   Digging coal, drilling for the precious oil,
   Nothing beats a hammer-hitting man.

JUST A CLOSER WALK WITH THEE

By
REV. EARL OSBORN

KEEP ON THE SUNNY SIDE

Arranged and Adapted by
SLIM MARTIN

Chorus:

you. Keep On The Sun - ny Side, Al - ways on the sun - ny side,

Keep On The Sun - ny Side of life; It will help us ev - 'ry day, It will

bright-en all the way, If we Keep On The Sun-ny Side of life.

2. Oh, the storm and its fury broke today,
   Crushing hopes that we cherish so dear;
   Clouds and storms will in time pass away,
   The sun again will shine bright and clear.
   Chorus

3. Let us greet with a song of hope each day,
   Though the moment be cloudy or fair;
   Let us trust in our Saviour away,
   Who keepeth ev'ry one in His care.
   Chorus

KENTUCKY BABE

by RICHARD BUCK
and ADAM GEIBEL

KICKIN' MULE

Arranged and Adapted by
SLIM MARTIN

As I went down to the huc-kle-ber-ry pic-nic Din-ner all o-ver the ground,

Skep-pers in the meat was nine foot deep, And the green flies walk-ing all a-round. The

bis-cuits in the o-ven was a-bak-ing, Beef-steak fry-ing in the pan,

Pret-ty gal sit-ting in the par-lour, Lord God A'-might-y, what a hand I stand!

Chorus:

Whoa there, mule, I tell you, Miss Li-za, you keep cool, I

ain't got time to kiss you now, I'm bus-y with this mule.

My uncle had an old mule,
His name was Simon Slick,
'Bove anything I ever did see
Was how that mule could kick.
Went to feed that mule one morning
And he met me at the door with a smile,
He backed one ear and he winked one eye
And he kicked me half a mile.
Chorus

LAREDO

Adapted by
BILL BRENNER

4. Get six of my buddies to carry my coffin,
   And six pretty maidens to sing a sad song,
   Take me to the valley and lay the sod o'er me,
   For I'm a young cowboy who played the game wrong."

5. "Oh, beat the drum slowly and play the fife lowly,
   And play the dead march as they carry my pall.
   Put bunches of roses all over my coffin,
   The roses will deaden the clods as they fall."

6. "Go gather around you a crowd of young cowboys,
   And tell them the story of this my sad fate.
   Tell one and the other before they go further,
   To stop their wild roving before it's too late."

7. "Go fetch me a cup, just a cup of cold water,
   To cool my parched lips," the cowboy then said.
   Before I returned, his brave spirit had left him,
   And, gone to his maker, the cowboy was dead.

The Streets of Laredo – 2

LIVE AND LET LIVE

By NAT BENTON

Chorus:

Live   And Let Live,   don't break   my heart,   Don't leave   me here   to

cry.   I   nev - er could live   if   we   should part,

Tell   me   you____ don't mean good - bye.

2. Stayed awake last night and I walked the floor,
   What makes you treat me so?
   Live and let live, don't break my heart,
   I don't want to live if you go.
   Chorus

3. You're the one who made me love you so,
   You're the one who's makin' me cry.
   You're the one who'd break my heart if you go,
   Tell me you don't mean good-bye.
   Chorus

IT'S HARD, AIN'T IT HARD?

By
WOODY HAYES

LIZA JANE

Adapted by
BILL BRENNER

LONESOME ROAD

Arranged and Adapted by
SLIM MARTIN

Look up and down that long, lone - some road,

Hang down your head _____ and cry, my Lord,

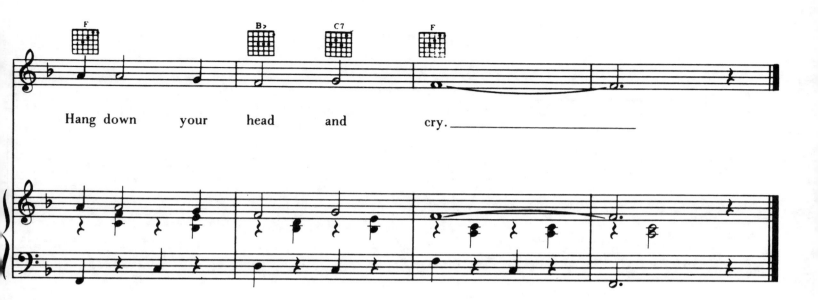

Hang down your head and cry. _____

2. They say all good friends must part some time,
   Why not you and I, my Lord,
   Who not you and I?

3. Oh, I wish to the Lord that I'd never been born,
   Or died when I was a baby, my Lord,
   Or died when I was a baby.

4. I would not be here eatin' this cold cornbread
   Or soppin' this salty gravy, my Lord,
   Or soppin' this salty gravy.

5. Oh, I wish to the Lord that I'd never seen your face,
   Or heard your lyin' tongue, my Lord,
   Heard your lyin' tongue.

6. You'd better look up and down that long lonesome road,
   Where all of your friends have gone, my Lord,
   And you and I must go.

7. You'd better look up and down that long lonesome road,
   Hang down your head and cry, my Lord,
   Hang down your head and cry.

LONG JOURNEY HOME
(TWO-DOLLAR BILL)

Adapted by CHARLIE SEATS

Chorus:

2. Black smoke a-risin', and it surely is a train,
   Surely is a train, Lord, it surely is a train.
   Black smoke a-risin', and it surely is a train.
   I'm on my long journey home.
   Chorus

3. I hear the train a-comin', and I'll soon be gone,
   Soon be gone, Lord, I'll soon be gone.
   I hear the train a-comin', and I'll soon be gone.
   I'm on my long journey home.
   Chorus

MAMA DON'T 'LOW

By
JIMMY MURRAY

3. Mama don't 'low no drums a-drummin' 'round here,
   No banjos, guitars a-strummin' 'round here,
   Well she's not here to rave and shout,
   And the Joneses living next door went out,
   Mama don't 'low no drums a-drummin' 'round here.

4. Mama don't 'low no loud mouth talkin' 'round here,
   Mama don't 'low no loud mouth talkin' 'round here,
   Well, I don't care what mama don't 'low,
   Gonna shoot my mouth off anyhow.
   Mama don't 'low no loud mouth talkin' 'round here.

5. Mama don't 'low no nuthin' going on here,
   Mama don't 'low no nuthin' going on here,
   Well, I don't see why my mama don't 'low,
   She was once as young as we are now,
   Mama don't 'low no nuthin' going on here.

MIDNIGHT SPECIAL

Adapted by
SAMMY CASH

2. Well if you're ever in Houston,
   You'd better walk on by
   Oh, you'd better not gamble, boy
   I say you'd better not fight.
   Well now, the sheriff, he'll grab you
   And his boys will pull you down
   And then before you know it
   You're penitentiary-bound.
      (To Chorus) A-let the Midnight Special etc.

3. Here comes Miss Lucy
   How in the world do you know?
   I know by her apron
   And by the dress she wore.
   An umbrella on her shoulder
   A piece of paper in her hand
   She gonna see the sheriff
   To try to free her man.
      (To Chorus) A-let the Midnight Special etc.

MOUNTAIN DEW

Adapted by
SLIM MARTIN

Moderately

Chorus:

They

call it that OLD MOUN-TAIN DEW, _____ And them that re-

fuse it are few. _____ You may go 'round the bend, but you'll

come back a-gain, For that good OLD MOUN-TAIN DEW. _____

MULE SKINNER BLUES

Adapted by
SAMMY CASH

PUTTING ON THE STYLE

Adapted by
SLIM MARTIN

real - ly have to smile, To see so man - y

peo - ple put - tin' on the style.

Verse:

1. Young man in a road - ster, Driv - ing like he's
2. La - dy wears a mink coat, Dia - monds 'round her

mad.   There's no doubt a - bout it,   He
wrist,   And her wealth - y es - cort   Adds

3. Take a look at Congress,
   Passing all those bills,
   Thinking they will cure us
   Of all the nation's ills.
   The way they promise plenty
   To all the rank and file,
   Pardon me, I call it:
   Puttin' on the style. (Chorus)

4. Preacher in the pulpit,
   Doctor by a bed,
   Lawyer in his office,
   Accountant in the red,
   Men who go a-courting,
   Women who beguile,
   Ev'rywhere you see folks
   Puttin' on the style. (Chorus)

5. Folks who go campaigning,
   Asking for your vote,
   Folks who keep explaining
   Things that Shakespeare wrote.
   Since the days of Cleo,
   Temptress of the Nile,
   Ev'rywhere we've had folks,
   Puttin' on the style. (Chorus)

NINE POUND HAMMER

Adapted by
JESSE WILLIAMS

OLD BLUE

Adapted by
SAM COOTS

3. I had an old dog, and his name was Blue,
   But he died and left me like he had to do,
   I said "Go on, Blue,
   I'm a-comin' too."

4. In Heaven some day, first thing I'll do,
   Gonna grab my horn and blow for Old Dog Blue
   I'll say "Come on, Blue,
   Fin'lly got here too."

5. I dug him a grave, and I put him down,
   And I carved a wooden marker which I bought in town,
   And I said "Old Blue,
   I'm a-comin' too."

OLD DAN TUCKER

Arranged and Adapted by
SLIM MARTIN

With Plenty of "Go"

1. I came to town ____ de ud-der night, I hear de noise, ___ den saw de fight, De
2. Old Dan-iel Tuck-er was a might-y man, He washed his face in a fry-ing pan, ____

watch-man was a-run-nin' 'roun', Cry-in' "Old Dan ___ Tuck-er's come to town". So
Combed his head wid a wag-on wheel, An' ___ died wid de tooth-ache in his heel. So

3. Old Dan Tucker's back in town,
    Swingin' the ladies all aroun':
    First to the right and then to the left,
    An' then to the gal that he loves best.

4. Old Dan Tucker he got drunk,
    He fell in de fire an' he kicked up a chunk;
    De red hot coals got in his shoe
    An' whee-wee! how de ashes flew.

5. Tucker is a nice old man,
    He us'd to ride our darby ram,
    He sent him whizzin' down de hill;
    If he hadn't got up, he'd laid dar still.

OLD JOE CLARK

Adapted by
SLIM MARTIN

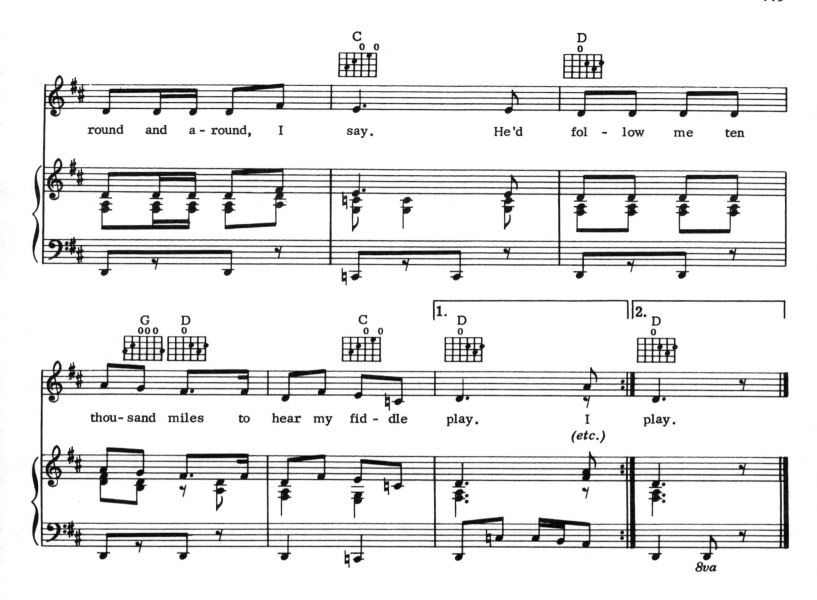

When I was a little boy,
I used to want a knife;
Now I am a bigger boy,
I only want a wife.

Wish I was a sugar tree,
Standin' in the middle of some town;
Ev'ry time a pretty girl passed,
I'd shake some sugar down.

Old Joe had a yellow cat,
She would not sing or pray;
She stuck her head in a buttermilk jar
And washed her sins away.

I wish I had a sweetheart;
I'd set her on the shelf,
And ev'ry time she'd smile at me
I'd get up there myself.

OLD RATTLER

Adapted by
SLIM MARTIN

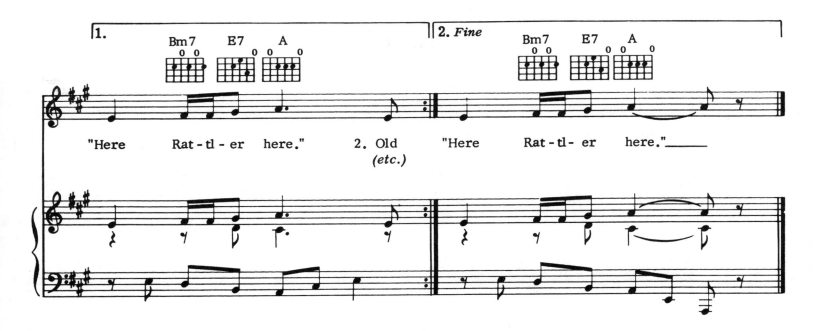

"Here Rat-tl-er here." 2. Old

(etc.)

"Here Rat-tl-er here."_____

Old Rattler treed the other night,
And I thought he treed a coon.
When I come to find out,
He was barkin' at the moon.

Well, Grandma had a yeller hen,
We set her, as you know.
We set her on three buzzard eggs
And hatched out one old crow.

Grandpa had a muley cow,
She's muley when she's born.
It took a jaybird forty years
To fly from horn to horn.

Now, if I had a needle and thread
As fine as I could sew,
I'd sew my sweetheart to my back
And down the road I'd go.

Old Rattler was a smart old dog,
Even though he was blind.
He wouldn't hurt one single thing
Though he was very fine.

One night I saw a big fat coon
Climb up in a tree.
I called Old Rattler right away
To git him down fer me.

But Rattler wouldn't do it
'Cause he liked that coon.
I saw them walkin' paw in paw
Later by the light of the moon.

Now Old Rattler's dead and gone
Like all good dogs do.
You better not act the dog yourself
Or you'll be goin' there too.

OLD SLEW FOOT

Adapted by RUSS MATHIS

big a-round the mid-dle and__ broad a-cross the rump, Run-ning nine-ty miles an ho-ur, Tak-ing

thir-ty feet a jump. Ain't nev-er been caught,__ He ain't nev-er been

treed, And some folks __ say he looks a lot __ like __ me.

2. Saved up my money and bought me some bees,
Started making honey way up in the trees.
Cut down the trees but the honey's all gone,
Old slew foot has done made himself at home.
Chorus

3. Winter's coming on and hits forty below.
River's froze over, so where can he go?
I'll chase him up the gulley and run him in the well,
Shoot him in the bottom just to listen to him yell.
Chorus

ON AND ON

by LESTER McGRATH

Moderately

Trav-'lin' down this long ___ and lone - some high-way, I'm so lone - some I could cry. Mem - o -ries ___ of how we once loved each oth - er, And ___ now you are say - ing good-

2. I've cried, I've cried, for you, my darlin',
   It breaks my heart to hear your name.
   My friends they all so loved you, my darlin',
   And they think that I'm to blame.
   Chorus

3. I had to follow you, my darlin',
   I can't see when the sun goes down.
   By your side is my destination,
   The road is clear, and that's where I'm bound.
   Chorus

On And On 2-2

POOR BOY

by J.D. CURTIS

1. As I went down to the riv - er, poor boy, To see the ships go by, ____ My sweet - heart stood on the deck of one, Where she waved to me "good - bye". ____

Bow down your head and cry, poor boy, Bow down your

head and cry, _____ And stop think-ing of that

wo-man you love, Bow down your head and cry. _____

2. She sailed away with a gambling man,
   Who had a false design.
   I knew that marriage was not his plan,
   He would ruin her life and mine.
   (Chorus)

3. I took a steamer to follow, poor boy,
   I searched in ev'ry port,
   And then one day very far away,
   There she was with her escort.
   (Chorus)

4. She said: "Oh please come no closer, poor boy,
   This man I can't resist."
   He came at me with a big jack-knife,
   And I met him with my fist.
   (Chorus)

5. We fought from morning till evening, poor boy,
   For the girl I might have wed,
   And he nicked my skin seven times, poor boy,
   Till I knocked him out, stone dead!
   (Chorus)

6. They took me down to the jail-house, poor boy,
   They'll never turn me loose.
   And they call this justice, poor boy, poor boy!
   Waiting for the hangman's noose.
   (Chorus)

7. I tried and failed for a pardon, poor boy!
   And so I have to die.
   My girl, she went back to New Orleans,
   But she waved to me "good-bye".
   (Chorus)

THE PREACHER AND THE BEAR

Adapted by
SONNY DAVIS

PRETTY POLLY

Arranged and Adapted by
SLIM MARTIN

Pol - ly, Pret - ty Pol - ly, come

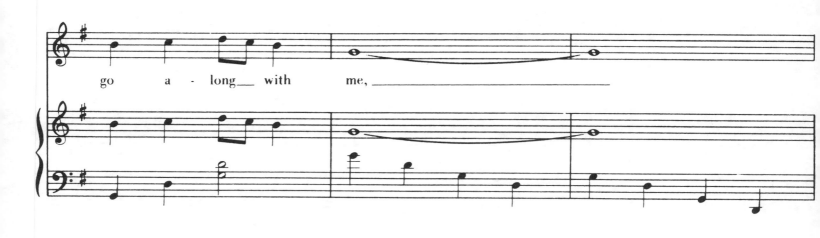

go a - long___ with me, _____

Pol - ly, _____ pret - ty Pol - ly, come

go a - long with me, Be - fore we get

Cm   D7   G

mar - ried, some pleas - ure to see.

2. Oh, Willy, little Willy, I'm afraid of your ways,
   Oh, Willy, little Willy, I'm afraid of your ways.
   The way you've been rambling, you'll lead me astray.

3. Oh, Polly, little Polly, your guess is about right,
   Oh, Polly, little Polly, your guess is about right.
   I dug on your grave in the heart of last night.

4. She knelt before him a-pleading for her life,
   She knelt before him a-pleading for her life,
   "Please let me be a single girl if I can't be your wife."

5. He stabbed her through the heart, her heart blood it did flow,
   He stabbed her through the heart, her heart blood it did flow,
   And into the grave pretty Polly did go.

6. Gentlemen and ladies, I'll bid you farewell,
   Gentlemen and ladies, I'll bid you farewell,
   For killin' pretty Polly will send my soul to hell.

ROCK ISLAND LINE

Adapted by
SLIM MARTIN

Fast

Chorus

I say the

ROCK IS - LAND LINE ___ is a might-y good road, ___ I say the Rock Is - land Line ___

___ is the road to ride, Oh the ROCK IS - LAND LINE ___ is a

might-y good road, ___ If you want to ride it, you will go like you're a -

2. Now this here train has but one design,
   To get you where you're going,
   The Rock Island Line! (Chorus)

3. And man, oh man! It's a place divine,
   For kissing in the tunnels
   The Rock Island Line! (Chorus)

4. Its destination ain't really mine,
   But anyhow, I'll take it,
   The Rock Island Line! (Chorus)

ROLL IN MY SWEET BABY'S ARMS

Adapted by
SLIM MARTIN

back then I'll roll in my sweet ba - by's

arms. bail.

Refrain:

Roll in my sweet baby's arms,
Roll in my sweet baby's arms,
Lay 'round the shack 'til the mail train comes back,
Then I'll roll in my sweet baby's arms.

Can't see what's the matter with my own true love,
She done quit writing to me,
She must think I don't love her like I used to,
Ain't that a foolish idea.

Sometimes there's a change in the ocean,
Sometimes there's a change in the sea,
Sometimes there's a change in my own true love,
But there's never no change in me.

Mama's a ginger-cake baker,
Sister can weave and can spin,
Dad's got an interest in that old cotton mill,
Just watch that old money roll in.

They tell me that your parents do not like me,
They have drove me away from your door,
If I had all my time to do over,
I would never go there any more.

Now where was you last Friday night,
While I was locked up in jail,
Walking the streets with another man,
Wouldn't even go my bail.

A ROVING GAMBLER

Adapted by
SAM COOTS

3. Had - n't been ___ in Wash - ing - ton for man - y more days than
7. "Would - n't mar - ry a farm - er, ___ he's al - ways in the

three, When I fell in love with a pret - ty lit - tle girl, and she
rain: ___ The man I want to mar - ry, wears a

fell in love with me. 4. She took me in her
great, big, gold, watch - chain." 8. "See the train a -

par - lor, She cooled me with her fan, She
com - in', she's com - in' 'round the curve, A -

140

RAILROAD BILL

Arranged and Adapted by
SLIM MARTIN

Rail - road Bill, Rail - road Bill, Live way up ___ on

Rail - road Hill, ___ Ride, ride, ___ ride. ride.

2. Railroad Bill, Railroad Bill,
He never work' and he never will,
Ride, ride, ride.

3. Kill me a chicken, send me the wing,
You think I'm workin', I don't do a thing,
Ride, ride, ride.

4. Railroad Bill, Railroad Bill,
Live way up on Railroad Hill,
Ride, ride, ride.

SALLY GOODIN

Arranged and Adapted by
SLIM MARTIN

Moderately

Had a piece of pie and I had a piece of pud-din', And I

gave it all a-way just to see my Sal-ly Good-in,

see my Sal-ly Good-in. Well, I looked down the road and I

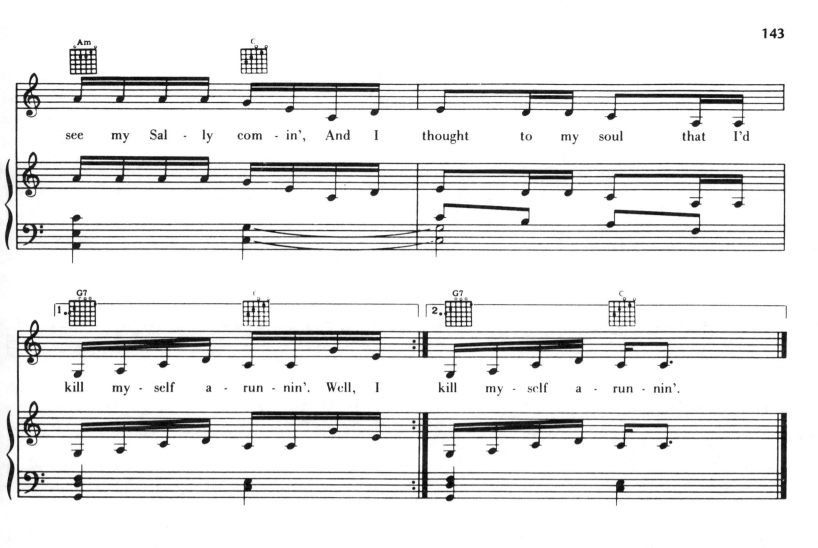

see my Sal - ly com - in', And I thought to my soul that I'd

kill my - self a - run - nin'. Well, I kill my - self a - run - nin'.

Love a 'tater pie and I love an apple puddin'

And I love a little girl that they call Sally Goodin. *Repeat*

But I dropped the 'tater pie and I left the apple puddin'

Cause I went across the mountain for to see my Sally Goodin. *Repeat*

Sally is my doxy and Sally is my daisy,

When Sally says she hates me I think I'm going crazy. *Repeat*

Little dog'll bark and the big dog'll bite you,

Little gal'll court you and the big gal'll fight you. *Repeat*

Raining and a-pouring and the creek's a-running muddy,

And I'm so drunk, Lord, I can't stand studdy. *Repeat*

I'm goin' up on the mountain and marry little Sally,

Raise corn on the hillside and the devil in the valley. *Repeat*

RYE WHISKY

Adapted by
SLIM MARTIN

Moderato, not too slowly

Rye whis-ky, rye whis-ky, rye whis-ky I cry. If I

don't get rye whis-ky I sure-ly will die. It's me.
(etc.)

It's whisky, rye whisky,
I know you of old,
You robbed my poor pockets
Of silver and gold.

It's beefsteak when I'm hungry,
Rye whisky when I'm dry,
A greenback when I'm hard up,
Oh, Heaven when I die.

I go to yonder holler
And I'll build me a still,
And I'll give you a gallon
For a five-dollar bill.

If the ocean was whisky
And I was a duck,
I'd dive to the bottom
And never come up.

But the ocean ain't whisky,
And I ain't a duck.
So I'll play Jack o' Diamonds
And trust to my luck.

Her parents don't like me,
They say I'm too poor,
And that I am unfit
To darken her door.

Her parents don't like me,
Well, my money's my own,
And them that don't like me
Can leave me alone.

Oh whisky, you villain,
You're no friend to me,
You killed my poor pappy,
God-damn you, try me.

SCARBOROUGH FAIR

Adaptation by
WOODY HAYES

SEE SEE RIDER
(C. C. RIDER)

Words and Music
by SONNY POTTER

SHORTY GEORGE

by DOC BENSON

SHADY GROVE

Arranged and Adapted by
SLIM MARTIN

Fast Dance

Peach - es in the sum - mer - time, Ap - ples in the fall, If I can't get the girl I love, Won't have none at all.

Chorus:

Shad - y grove, my true love, Shad - y grove, I know

Shad - y grove, my true love, I'm bound for the Shad - y grove.

2. Once I was a little boy,
   Playin' in the sand,
   Now I am a great big boy,
   I think myself a man.
   Chorus

3. When I was a little boy,
   I wanted a whittlin' knife;
   Now I am a great big boy,
   An' I want a little wife.
   Chorus

4. Wish I had a banjo string,
   Made of golden twine,
   And every tune I'd pick on it—
   Is "I wish that girl were mine".
   Chorus

6. Ev'ry night when I go home,
   My wife, I try to please her,
   The more I try, the worse she gets,
   Damned if I don't leave her.
   Chorus

7. Fly around, my blue-eyed girl,
   Fly around, my daisy,
   Fly around, my blue-eyed girl,
   Nearly drive me crazy.
   Chorus

8. The very next time I go that road
   And it don't look so dark and grazy,
   The very next time I come that road,
   I'll stop and see my daisy.
   Chorus

SHENANDOAH

by JIM O'NEAL

1. Oh SHEN - AN - DOAH, I long to
2. Oh SHEN - AN - DOAH, I love to your

hear you, A - way you roll - ing
daught - er, A - way you roll - ing

riv - er, _____ Oh SHEN - AN - DOAH, _____ I long to
riv - er, _____ Oh SHEN - AN - DOAH, _____ I love to your

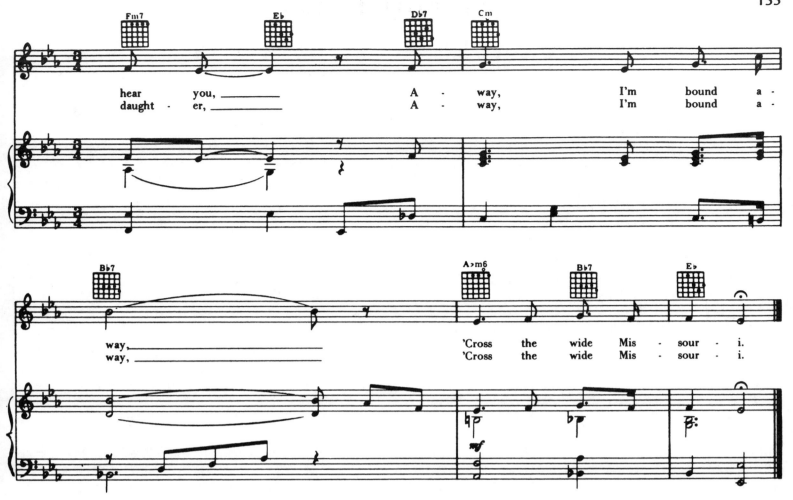

3. 'Tis seven long years since last I saw you,
    Away, you rolling river,
    'Tis seven long years since last I saw you,
    Away, I'm bound away,
    'Cross the wide Missouri.

4. Oh Shenandoah, I love your daughter,
    Away, you rolling river,
    Oh Shenandoah, I'll come to claim her,
    Away, I'm bound away,
    'Cross the wide Missouri.

5. In all these years, whene'er I saw her,
    We have kept our love a secret,
    Oh! Shenandoah, I do adore her,
    Away, I'm bound away,
    'Cross the wide Missouri.

6. Oh Shenandoah, she's bound to leave you,
    Away, you rolling river,
    Oh Shenandoah, I'll not deceive you,
    Away, I'm bound away,
    'Cross the wide Missouri.

SHORT'NIN' BREAD

Adapted by
BILL BRENNER

SHUCKIN' THE CORN

Arranged and Adapted by
SLIM MARTIN

1. I have a ship on the o-cean, _____ All lined with
2. The wind blows cold in _____ Cai-ro, _____ The sun re -

sil - ver and gold. _____ Be - fore I'd see my
-fus - es to shine. _____ Be - fore I'd see my

true love suf-fer, That ship should be an-chored and sold._____
true love suf-fer, I'd work all the sum-mer time._____

Chorus:

I'm a-go-in' to the shuck-in' of the corn, _____ I'm a-go-in' to the

shuck-in' of the corn, _____ A - shuck-in' of the corn and a-

blow-in' of the horn, I'm a-go-in' to the shuck-in' of the corn._____

Shuckin' the Corn 2-2

SWEET THING

by JOHN THOMAS

Medium Tempo

mf

Sweet Thing, I'm writ-ing this let-ter to you, Your name will be

blot-ted with tears._____ Please read it and an-swer, and tell me it's

true, Your love will ____ re-main through the __ years._____

I want to be loved, but only by you,
That's why tonight I'm so sad.
I know that another has gained that reward,
A love that I wanted so bad.

Chorus

TAKE MY RING FROM YOUR FINGER

Arranged and Adapted by
SLIM MARTIN

Moderately

I'm ___ hap-py now at last you are smil-ing, ___ And I'm

glad I have found you in his arms, For no long - er I'll keep you un-

hap-py ___ And I'll vow to nev-er do you an-y harm.

Chorus:

Take My Ring From Your Fin - ger,___ Set me free ___ as a

dove, You don't need me no long - er

You have found the one you love.

So my heart will likely break when I leave you,
When my position at last I can see.
When I found you in his arms you were crying,
And that's more than you ever did for me.
Chorus

You can have our little home in the mountains,
With the honeysuckles twining 'round the door.
When he carries you over the threshold,
I hope that you'll be happy evermore.
Chorus

TEN THOUSAND MILES

Adapted by
JERRY KNOTT

Ten Thousand Miles — 2

THAT'S WHERE MY MONEY GOES

Adapted by
DUSTY HOFFMAN

3. That's where my money goes,
My girl turns up her nose -
At anything that's cheap,
For instance, she froze -
When, on a luncheon date,
It was hot dogs we ate,
Say, boys, that's where my money goes!

4. That's where my money goes,
Taking her out to shows,
Love can be quite expensive,
This lover knows.
And yet my heart will sing -
When she accepts my ring,
Say, boys, that's where my money goes!

5. That's where my money goes,
One thing before I close:
Love may be lovely but it
Sure has its woes.
My suit is old and torn,
Five years my shoes are worn,
You know just where my money goes!

SOURWOOD MOUNTAIN

by LEWIS ALISON

2. I call my darling a blue eyed daisy,
   Hey! Hey! Deedee um day.
   If she won't have me, I'll sure go crazy,
   Hey! Hey! Deedee um day.
   I got to have my blue eyed daisy,
   If she refuses, I'll go crazy,
   I got to have my blue eyed daisy,
   Hey! Hey! Deedee um day.

3. Ducks go a-simming across the river,
   Hey! Hey! Deedee um day.
   And in the winter, we sure do shiver,
   Hey! Hey! Deedee um day.
   Duck go a-swimming across the river,
   And in the winter, we sure do shiver,
   I like the living on Sourwood Mountain,
   Hey! Hey! Deedee um day.

THIS TRAIN

Adapted by
JESSE WILLIAMS

TRAV'LIN' MAN

by MARTY WILLIAMS

SALTY DOG

Adapted by
JESSE WILLIAMS

TURKEY IN THE STRAW

Adapted by
JESSE WILLIAMS

tur-key in the hay
roll 'em up and twist 'em up a high tuck-a-haw, and__ hit 'em up a tune__ called__
"Tur-key in the Straw!" Oh I (etc.)
"Tur-key in the Straw!"

Came to the river and I couldn't get across
Paid five dollars for an old blind hoss
Wouldn't go ahead, nor he wouldn't stand still
So he went up and down like an old saw mill.

As I came down the new cut road
Met Mr. Bullfrog, met Miss Toad
And every time Miss Toad would sing
Ole Bullfrog cut a pigeon wing.

Oh, I jumped in the seat, and I gave a little yell,
The horses run away, broke the wagon all to hell;
Sugar in the gourd and honey in the horn,
I never was so happy since the hour I was born.

UNDER THE DOUBLE EAGLE

By JOSEF WAGNER

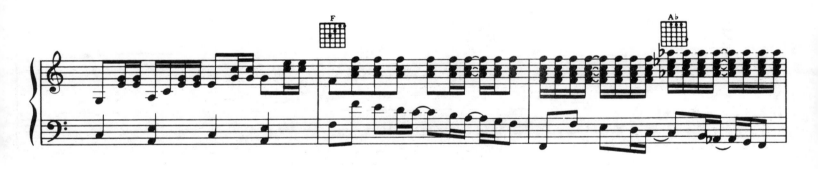

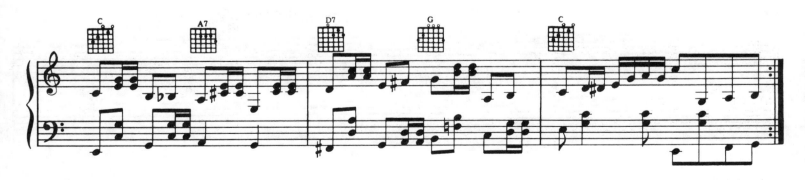

Under the Double Eagle 2-2

USED-TO-BE

By JACK CARTER

Moderately

You don't love me an - y - more, my dar - lin' __ I'm just a used - to - be to you. Those cold, cold kiss - es that you gave __ me lit - tle dar - lin', __ Proves that you __ found some - bod - y

Chorus:

new.   To - mor-row'll   be   an - oth - er   lone - some

day _____   And I   know you'll want me   far   a -

way._____   You   don't love me   an - y -

more,   my dar - lin' __   I'm   just a used - to - be to   you.

Used to Be 2-2

THE WABASH CANNONBALL

Adapted by
JESSE WILLIAMS

1. From the great At-lan-tic O-cean to the wide Pa-cif-ic's shore, From the ones we leave be-hind us to the ones we see once more. She's might-y tall and hand-some, and quite well known by all, How we love the choo choo of the WA-BASH CAN-NON-

2. Lis-ten to the rhyth-mic jin-gle and the rum-ble and the roar, As she glides a-long the wood-lands thro' the hills and by the shore. You hear the might-y en-gine and pray that it won't stall, While we safe-ly trav-el on the WA-BASH CAN-NON-

3. She was com-ing from At-lan-ta on a cold De-cem-ber day. As she rolled in-to the sta-tion, I could hear a wom-an say: He's might-y big and hand-some, and sure did make me fall," "He's a-com-ing tow'rd me on the WA-BASH CAN-NON-

THE WAYFARIN' STRANGER

Adapted by
JESSE WILLIAMS

WHERE I'M BOUND

Arranged and Adapted by
SLIM MARTIN

It's a   long and dust-y road, it's a   hot and heav-y load, And the   peo - ple that you meet aren't al-ways

kind,   Some are   bad,   some are good, some have   done the best they could; Some have

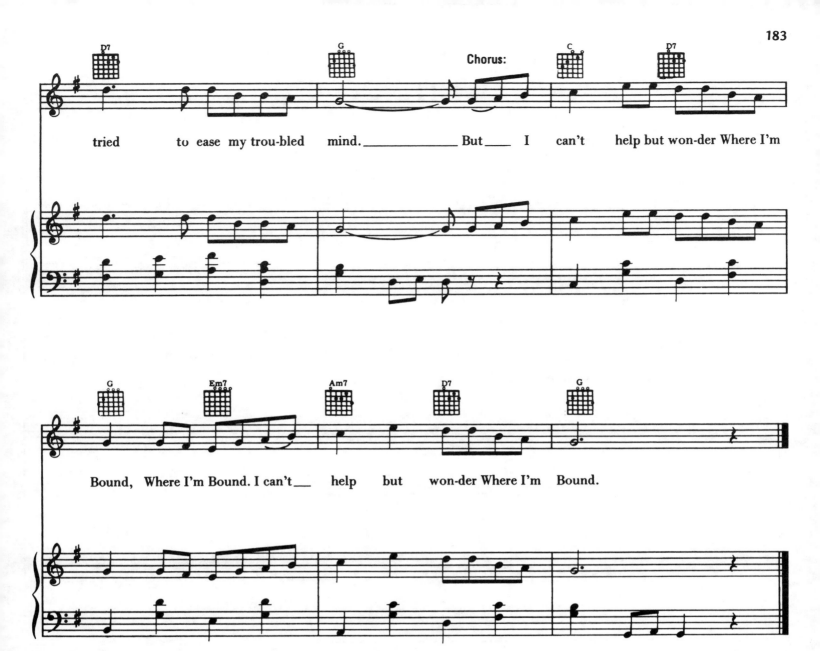

2. I have been around this land just doing the best I can,
   Trying to find what I was meant to do.
   And the faces that I see are as worried as can be,
   And I think that they are wondering too.
   Chorus

3. I had a buddy way back home, till he started out to roam,
   Now I hear he's out by 'Frisco Bay.
   Sometimes when I've had a few, his voice comes singing through,
   And I'm going out to see him some old day.
   Chorus

4. If you see me passing by and you sit and wonder why
   You weren't meant to be a rambler too.
   Nail your shoes to the kitchen floor, lace them up, and bar the door,
   And thank the stars for the roof that's over you.
   Chorus

Where I'm Bound 2-2

WHITE DOVE

By DOC BENSON

With Feeling

In the deep roll-ing hills__ of old Vir - gin - ia, There's a place that I love__ so well, _____ Where I spent man-y days _____ of my child-hood__ In the cab-in that we loved so ___ well.

Chorus:

White

Dove will moan in sor - row, The wil - lows will hang their __ heads._____ I live my life in sor - row _____ Since Moth - er and Dad - dy are dead.

2. We were all so happy there together
In our peaceful, little mountain home,
But the Saviour needs angels in heaven,
Now they sing around the great white throne.
Chorus

3. As the years go by I often wonder
If we will all be together someday,
And each night as I wander to the graveyard
Darkness finds me as I kneel to pray.
Chorus

WILL THE CIRCLE BE UNBROKEN?

Moderato

by SARAH MILLS

1. There are loved ones in the glo - ry Whose dear forms you oft - en miss.
2. joy - ous days of child - hood Oft they told of won - drous love.
3. mem - ber songs of heav - en which you sang with child - ish voice.
4. pic - ture hap - py gath - 'rings 'round the fire - side long a - go,
5. one their seats were emp - tied, One by one they went a - way.

When you close your earth - ly sto - ry Will you
Point - ed to the dy - ing Sav - iour, Now they
Do you love the hymns they taught you, Or are
And you think of tear - ful part - ings When they
Now the fam - i - ly is part - ed. Will it

THE WRECK OF THE OLD 97

Adapted by
JESSE WILLIAMS

Well, they gave him his or-ders at Mon - roe, Vir - gin - ia, say - in' "Steve, you are way be - hind time. This is not 'thir - ty - eight,' but it's old 'nine - ty - sev - en.' You must

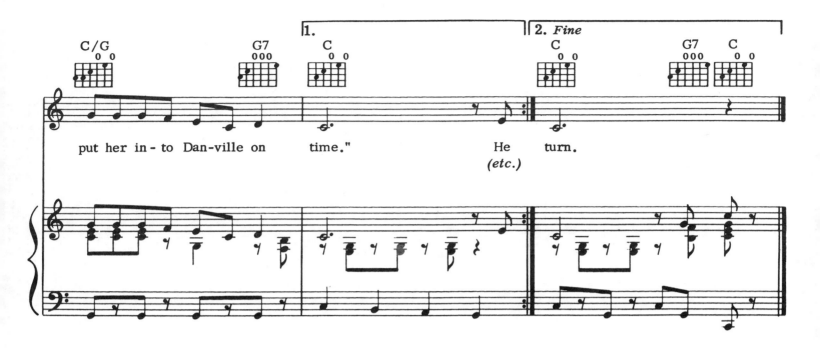

put her in-to Dan-ville on time."   He turn.
(etc.)

He turned and said to his black greasy fireman,
"Just shovel on a little more coal,
And when we cross the White Oak Mountain
You can watch old 'ninety-seven' roll."

It's a mighty rough road from Lynchburg to Danville,
On a line on a three mile grade,
It was on this grade that he lost his average,
You can see what a jump he made.

He was going down the grade makin' ninety miles an hour,
When his whistle broke into a scream,
They found him in the wreck
With his hand on the throttle, he was scalded to death by the steam.

Now, ladies, you must take warning,
From this time now on learn,
Never speak harsh words to your true loving husband,
He may leave you and never return.

ROCKY TOP

Words and Music by
Boudleaux Bryant and Felice Bryant

Lively

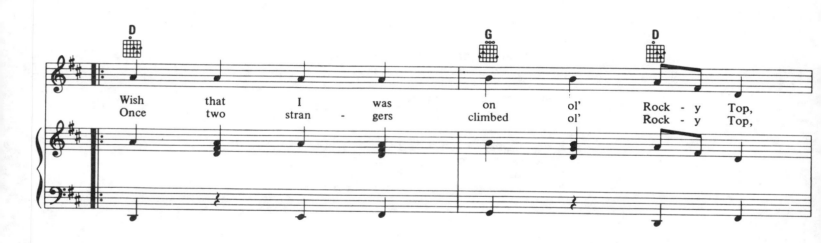

Wish that I was on ol' Rock-y Top,
Once two stran-gers climbed ol' Rock-y Top,

down in the Tenn-es-see hills; Ain't no smog-gy
look-in' for a moon-shine still; Stran-gers ain't come

Verse 3:
I've had years of cramped-up city life
Trapped like a duck in a pen;
All I know is it's a pity life
Can't be simple again. (Chorus)